Rational Universalism

The Second Directive

A NEW VIEW OF LIFE AFTER DEATH
AND OUR SPIRITUAL EVOLUTION

by

Barry Wachs, Ph.D.

CCB Publishing
British Columbia, Canada

Rational Universalism, The Second Directive:
A New View of Life After Death and Our Spiritual Evolution

Copyright ©2012 by Barry Wachs, Ph.D.
ISBN-13 978-1-927360-82-8
First Edition

Library and Archives Canada Cataloguing in Publication
Wachs, Barry, 1944-
Rational universalism, the second directive : a new view of life after death and our spiritual evolution / by Barry Wachs – 1st ed.
ISBN 978-1-927360-82-8
Also available in electronic format.
1. Future life. 2. Religion and science.
I. Title. II. Title: Second directive.
BL535.W33 2012   202'.3   C2012-904766-X

Extreme care has been taken to ensure that all information presented in this book is accurate and up to date at the time of publishing. Neither the author nor the publisher can be held responsible for any errors or omissions. Additionally, neither is any liability assumed for damages resulting from the use of the information contained herein.

All rights reserved. No part of this publication may be reproduced, stored in a retrieval system or transmitted in any form or by any means, electronic, mechanical, photocopying, recording or otherwise without the express written permission of the publisher. Printed in the United States of America, the United Kingdom and Australia.

Publisher: CCB Publishing
             British Columbia, Canada
             www.ccbpublishing.com

Dedicated to all the flawed yet evolving souls

Preface

What motivated me to write a book on religion? It's obvious upon visitation to any library or bookstore that there is certainly no shortage of theories or analyses of religions and/or religious doctrine. There are so many selling their particular view or opinion or research on the subject.

I have been, like so many of my generation, in search of the truth. We've become disenchanted with or disenfranchised from, our traditional religious roots, especially in the Judeo-Christian teachings. Then, of course, there are those born again, who have marched blindly and proudly into the abyss of dogmatic acceptance and staunch defense of their bible, Koran, Torah or New Testament.

In John Bradshaw's book "The Family," he talks about the rules of total obedience which children are forced to accept through guilt, fear and intimidation. He talks about the family rules, like the "no talk" rule, where children should be seen and not heard, etc. Total obedience to the parent ultimately deifies the parent who assumes that these powers over the child are God given. Bradshaw quotes Alice Miller, a Swiss psychiatrist, who developed the concept of

Poisonous Pedagogy in which society sees a good child as meek, agreeable, considerate, and unselfish. Adults are seen as masters of the dependent child and parents determine in a "godlike fashion" what is right and wrong. All this leads to child shame, compulsivity, repression of free thought and feelings, and the blind acceptance of beliefs. It should be obvious that, once grown, the "adult child" carries this repression and guilt with him as well as a realization that his parents are only human and therefore imperfect, so he turns to an idealized spiritual mystical parent who has filled his early childhood in terms of religion and faith. This mystical parent doles out reward and punishment for the acts of the new adult, their children and all future generations. The "insidiousness of total obedience" first to our original parents, then to the Mystical father, leads to the expectation of "obedience, rigidity, orderliness, denial of feelings, and to a society, easily manipulated and led by fear, promises of reward, forgiveness, and guilt."

We must balance out ultimate authoritarianism of the parent, society and religion, in favor of freedom of thoughts and feelings. This is an enlightened view of the social and religious order. This is the biggest threat to established religious doctrine and power.

In this humble set of essays, I will put forth a theory and concept that could be acceptable to all. My intention is not to dispel someone's belief, but rather to meld the obvious proofs of science with that of faith; offering a logical explanation and rationalization for one's faith and beliefs as viewed from a scientific background. We can become free from authoritarianism and blind faith by providing a basis for belief that is rational.

When all is said and done, I am hopeful that those who can embrace this theory (which is, as we will see, all that it can be) will be perfectly comfortable within their own set of beliefs, dogma and religious practices. They will know that there is a rational basis for their beliefs and they will no longer have to defend, proselytize, or question them.

I am not writing this for profit or fame, but simply to share the message and lessons that have come to me. I make no claim of burning bushes or voices from afar, only my years of learning, hurting, healing, loving, fearing, caring, experiencing, and sensing from an intuitive place that there is indeed more. Perhaps now at age 67, I have come to this as recognition of my own mortality. This is not meant to be autobiographical so I won't bore you with how I came to this place in life. Simply put, as a man, I experienced child rearing as the normal path to immortality, but something inside me is driving me to give birth to something even grander. Behold my child--"Rational Universalism, The Second Directive"--spawned from the fertilization of the flagellate of science with the ovum of religion and faith. It is up to you, the reader, to determine how you will care for this child; with understanding and love, allowing it to grow and mature, or to ignore it as just another religious mutation.

I am writing this, not to change or challenge your beliefs but rather, to offer an opportunity to view them from a slightly different point of view; one which will carry you and your soul into the future.

Barry Wachs

Contents

Preface v
Chapter I: *In the Beginning* 1
Chapter II: *Definition* 11
Chapter III: *Energy and Space* 17
Chapter IV: *The Justification of Existence* 25
Chapter V: *The Leap* 31
Chapter VI: *The Gift* 37
Chapter VII: *The Second Directive Revealed* 41
Chapter VIII: *The Do's and Doesn'ts* 47
Chapter IX: *Synthesis* 53
About the Author 58

We have a window of opportunity, to stop battling for supremacy of belief, and to embrace a new paradigm based on science, which can at the same time support faith.

Chapter I

In the Beginning

Life force was set into motion. It makes no difference whether it was Big Bang or by Design, only that it began.

I choose not to be drawn into the debate of how life began, as it is only a matter of group or individual Ego, as to who is right. For our lives today, what does it matter? What really matters is how we live our lives in the present, not to win some esoteric debate for the sake of winning. Do we need to kill, maim, reject, destroy, distrust, or fear someone or some other group so that we can claim we are the winner of the creation debate? When we fly a victory flag because we have won, vanquished, or destroyed in the name of our own belief system, this flies in the face of the evolution of our own spirit and soul, the life force, and even God as we each define it. (Note: I give God no gender identity; that's up to you.)

What is important about Life is that Life Force was set into motion. It makes no difference if it was Big Bang or by Design; only that it began. Darwin is indisputable, except to those who seek to gain power, control or money from questioning it. The Scopes trial has long since passed. I will not argue or debate the beginning or what set evolution into motion. Intelligent Design is just as good an explanation as any; you can make that decision individually. Just accept that the evolutionary process began, even if was primordial ooze from some unknown source, an accident of amino acids, or some divine intervention.

Instead let's fast-forward through the evolutionary history of man, to the time when we evolved from the Cro-Magnon man to the model of the modern-day Homo sapiens. Suddenly, the primitive tribal model that existed became much more organized. Social, cultural, political and spiritual concerns began to take form. Man was thrust out of the garden of innocence into a much more complicated society with responsibilities and alliances. Hunting and gathering, so that the tribe would survive and prosper as an entity, became a way of life for the early tribes.

It is in this setting that I wish to focus my attention on the spiritual evolution of faith and religion. I ask and for good reason, what was it that created the initial and primary development of belief and faith? I have asked many people and almost everyone gives me a similar answer. Faith evolved out of a fear of, or a respect for, the unknown, the mystical powers of the universe, as seen in daily life, from birth to death, from weather to environment .primitive man had no explanation and therefore assigned it to the unanswerable. Throughout the history of man, giving names, identities, even iconic stature, to the mystical powers with hopes that these entities could somehow influence, change or modify our lives, weather, birth, death, or environments, etc.

Now let us imagine 6,000 or 7,000 years ago, maybe 10,000 years ago, the tribe was out hunting and gathering. They identified a person, man or woman, in the tribe who took it upon themselves to be the keeper of the faith, as a shaman, a healer, a witchdoctor. The tribe was too busy hunting and gathering to be involved with the Gods, so the shaman took on the duties of keeping the tribe connected on a daily or weekly basis. The tribe would come to the shaman's cave or campfire every Sunday to be reconnected. For that service, the tribe would give the shaman some of the food they'd hunted and gathered. (I like to call it the "meat and wheat.") The shaman was starting to collect a reasonable quantity of meat and wheat. A great deal of power was starting to coalesce in the cave of the shaman.

Well, guess what happened? The chief/leader didn't like that very much. He began to question the power of the shaman and the shaman's intent; so one day he came knocking on the shaman's door. "Mr. Shaman," he said, "Do you want to live until tomorrow?" Well, you know the answer; of course, he/she did. Well, guess what he said? "You will now make me chief/leader of our tribe with a direct line (lineage) to the Gods. It is through my lineage and grace that the Gods grant you your power. I am now the way to God(s), via your teachings and beliefs."

It is with this unholy alliance that the world entered into

theocracy as a means to reach the Gods, and to manipulate and control the tribe through fear of the unknown and the reaction of the Gods through the Chief. Do it my way, or die!!!! "Follow my laws, which I and the Shaman have been given from the Gods, or else." So the alliance between the shaman and the politician occurred, and a complicated code of behavior followed.

If the poor, unsuspecting tribesmen broke those codes, they would suffer untold acts at the hands of the chief and the shaman as allegedly dictated by the Gods. Thousands of years passed; laws, codes, stories, folktales, oral history evolved until writing was created, at which time, laws and codes became written down, solidified. Soon, they became the law of the land, administered always by a chief and a shaman of one sort or another. As populations and cultures grew, so did the powers of the theocracy, grounded in fear of the unknown, the mystical, and controlled by the codified beliefs as created by the chiefs and the shamans for control and power. This is still the primary model of most of our societies today. We need only to look at the American politic and the re-emergence of the religious right to see how quickly the politician turns to religion for power.

Now don't misunderstand me; I do not want to discount the importance of codes of behavior and ethics that religion and faith have created to allow civilization to function. One only need look at the basic Ten Commandments, if nothing else, as a guide for us to live with one another.

I must take a moment to give homage to George Carlin, one of the great comedians of the 20th century, who wrote a telling analysis of the Ten Commandments, in which he boils the 10 down to three and states that the rest was just hype designed to control and manipulate the masses. Basically they are as follows:

1) **Always be honest and faithful**
2) **Try not to kill anyone unless they pray to a different avenging God than you pray to.**
3) **Keep your religion to yourself!**

A paraphrased excerpt from George Carlin's *When Will Jesus Bring the Pork Chops* (2004)

Laws are needed to maintain order in a civilization. It is when those laws are tied to belief and consequences from the mystical unknown as opposed to civil response that we begin to be manipulated and controlled by theocracy or theocratic concepts. Every church, mosque, synagogue, faith, and religion is a micro theocracy. They do not like to give up power or control and will therefore go to almost any length necessary to maintain and survive in order to perpetuate their belief system, including manipulate their followers, almost always with guilt and fear. These actions became justified so that a given belief system could continue, grow in numbers and survive.

It is in this context that my theory begins to unfold and to make sense. As science, logic, and rational thought began to emerge during the Reformation, some of these belief systems began to lose their luster. Always lurking behind the scenes were the power brokers and religious institutions who refused to surrender their grip on the populace. They created stronger rules, punishments, and consequences from the God(s) if their laws, rules and codes were broken, brain washing and frightening their sheep even more so. Generations of people were made to believe in irrational, illogical thinking processes until it became ingrained in their very essence, from birth to death. Questioning it meant death and "damnation," excommunication, shunning and rejection, being cast out into the hard, cruel world alone.

As science and rational thought continued to emerge, the Powers That Be had to create a sense that science was the enemy of faith; so science became the scapegoat. If the theocracy could turn the people against science and rational thought, as destroyers of the faith, they could deflect their perceived attack on their belief systems and their control.

I am here to say that science is neutral in this debate. It was never the purpose of science to debunk or destroy faith, but only to enlighten, to learn, and to understand the natural world. The world is not flat! We understand that. The theocracy only accepts what it perceives scientifically neutral and rejects what may be considered an attack on its basis for existence. It fights against Darwinism, and yet ignores the obvious embryological development we can see in any such lab. It accepts creating hybrid flowers or foodstuffs. One of their own monks, Mendel, began the earliest demonstrations of this, yet they refuse to apply it to the human condition. How much longer do the masses have to suffer from the oppressiveness of the theocracies and their abuse of science?

I want to clear up something. I am not against an enlightened theocracy. We as humans derive a great deal from the organizational presence of the theocracies. We have order, ethics, and rules for living together as cultures and societies. There is social comfort, a sense of familiarity that appeals to our family/tribal model. There is support in a hostile world: a place to teach our young about the good and positive in the world; a place to go when life is hard or hands us obstacles. It has been a bastion for the arts and creativity, and yes, even learning and experimentation as long as it did not threaten the basic core folklore of the theocracy. Finally, it does what it was always meant to do, it attempt to connect us to the mystical and unknown.

So here is where I truly began this quest for an answer. How can faith and science reconcile? Where is the common ground upon which we can build a new paradigm? How can we bring these two forces together without what appears to destroy the very foundations of faith and belief, retaining a respect for the what the theocracy has done and can continue to provide the masses; and at the same time, understanding that science marches forth and is ever changing, and evolving our understanding of the universe and the natural world?

So I present *Rational Universalism, The Second Directive*; the alchemy of faith and science, a new view of the mystical and unknown, one which can be adopted by science to prove or disprove, and by the theocracies to bolster their institutions without fear of losing control.

Barry Wachs

Rational Universalism, The Second Directive

Rational Universalism is the acceptance on a soul level, that there is no separation in reality, but only in Ego, and that to the extent that we connect to the Energy of the Universe is the measure of our inner peace, enlightenment and power.

Chapter II

Definition

I see the Universe as a giant organism in which we each share in its vitality, its energy, its past, present and future.

Let us begin with the definition of Rational Universalism. This is an important step because its root brings forth images of existing church doctrines such as Unitarian, Unity, Christ Unity, etc. As in all discussions of faith, there will be some overlapping for reasons that should be obvious as we develop this theory.

The concept of the Universe, as we know it, is far beyond our logical mind. Concepts of time, space, and distances are truly for the astro-physician, quantum theory, and clergy. The Universe represents the ultimate unknown. There have been many theories proposed including parallel realities, etc. I will make no attempt to enter this debate as the answer lies in faith and what we can experience with our five senses, assistive technology such as telescopes, etc., and mathematics.

The Rational Universalism I propose relates to our place in the Universe as opposed to the Universe itself. Rational

Universalism invites the acceptance that we are all part of, and connected to, the Universe. I see the Universe as a giant organism in which we each share in its vitality, its energy, its past, present and future. Not only do we share it with the Macro Universe, but with every organic and inorganic object and asset within the universe.

Oneness is not a new concept. Almost every religion we can name has an element of oneness. In Zen they talk about being one with a given object or condition or circumstance. In the Judeo Christian beliefs, they talk of oneness with God. In the Moslem system, it is oneness with Allah. Jung called it the collective consciousness; Plato, world soul.

What is important here, is to recognize that it makes no difference what we call it; it is all oneness with the Universe. We are truly, organically, atomically and energetically one with the Universe. We are the Universe. We simply manufacture separateness to define our egos and to create an identity for perceived survival. We do this because of the vastness of the universe. It is too much for us to take the responsibility for the Universe and to conceive that we are vessels for all that is, was and will be. In order to maintain our own sanity, we create this definition of our institutions and ourselves. We focus on the small picture, because the big picture is too big, too insecure, too fearful, and………uncontrollable. Make no mistake, we are one, even though we choose to tune out our energetic receptors.

It is in the pursuit of reconnecting with the energy of the Universe that we begin our search for that which has been identified as inspiration, godliness, connection, spiritual identification, out of body, inner peace, Nirvana, enlightenment, Chi. I believe we are initially born with it but, in the name of survival, we lose contact with it.

If we can accept that all institutions and religious beliefs begin with the reconnection, the coming, then it is only a small step to accepting that all paths lead to Nirvana, to truth. If we can put aside our need for ego and definition through our own religious practices and understand that all beliefs, practices, and religions are one, then defense and missionary zeal are unnecessary. If we accept that we are all brothers and sisters, uncles and aunts, that we may not live in the same house, but we are all in the same neighborhood, working for the same good in the long run, in search of the same inner peace and happiness, in our own way; we do not have to create the energetic separation for our own identification.

We can then begin to recognize the difference between real faith and belief and manipulation for power and control. We should then be able to agree that it is not important how someone else worships or seeks connection to the mystical powers, but instead be concerned only with our own personal connection to the God Force/Life Force. It is so easy for us to slip into primitive competition scripts and project them onto our religious affiliations and, in turn, gain some kind of ego gratification about being bigger, better, more righteous, more correct, or being and knowing "the way". We can put the missionary testosterone away; it need not apply.

Barry Wachs

Rational Universalism, The Second Directive

One God, one soul, one spirit, many universes, it is to that understanding of our place and order that we strive for connection. It is in the fear of that loss, that we are vulnerable to manipulation.

Chapter III

Energy and Space

We are not separate from him, her or it. We are an integral part of ….God…It is in that connection that we ultimately experience inner peace.

It's important to begin this discussion with the dismantling of the common concept of space. What I'm suggesting is that what we view as open space between objects and people is simply a perception. In reality, the space we create perceptually is filled with atoms, molecules and energy; there is no void or vacuum, but rather a definition of density as opposed to emptiness. Our egos need to create this artificial separation between objects so that we can define them as they exist in our reality. It doesn't take much to understand that if, in fact, there is no space and that all objects inert and organic are connected to each other by this atomic and energetic field, then we are all part of the same organism separated only by distance and time, not space.

Everything and everyone in the universe is connected on some level. This is indisputable except in those rare conditions, perhaps in outer space where a pure vacuum exists. Where the difficulty enters into the discussion is exactly what kind of energy is this that binds the Universe together? We know it's there; scientifically, we know the molecules and atoms of hydrogen, carbon, oxygen, etc. are in the air, but what energy source not only binds those molecules to the air but also binds us to them? How is that connection made? Surely, we can concede that we too are made of atoms and molecules and energy of similar nature just re-arranged; and that our skin, which is highly permeable, acts only as a visual barrier, not an actual barrier to that same atomic energy.

So, are you mentally ready to take the next, really big step? If, in the biblical sense, we are connected with all matter, living, dead, past, present and future, ad infinitum, then doesn't it seem clear that whatever you choose to perceive as God--and I make no attempt to break down or change your individual concept--that we are all part and parcel of that God. We are not separate from him, her or it; we are an integral part of the God organism, connected in the same way we are connected to the entire universe.

Consider for a moment the law of conservation of energy which states that energy, like matter, cannot be created nor destroyed, but only changes form. Scientifically, we have identified many types of energy. Some of the most common being electrical, chemical, mechanical, potential or kinetic, fission, fusion, atomic, hydroelectric, solar, etc. The common thread amongst the identified energies is that we have at one time or another harnessed these energies, controlled them, and used them. Man has manipulated, produced (from one source to another) and otherwise defined these energies by their means of production, use, conductivity, and outcome.

In quantum physics, however, we can begin to question the relationship between energy and matter. The theory of relativity states that mass and energy are equivalent and that one can be converted to the other. In quantum theory we recognize that energy can demonstrate itself as particle (or mass) and as wave, and can and does flow directionally.

All of this confirms Plato's concept that the world, soul and body cannot be separated, as does the Hindu image of the Brahman or "world soul." The German philosophers from the Kant school, Fiche and Von Schelling, joined Plato in concept by defining the "Anima Mendi" which is the organizing spirit or soul, that acts as a unifying principle of the universe.

Given that we are all connected, all part of God/Life Energy, we therefore all possess the ability to affect the atomic energetic field of which we are a part. All that we do, or don't do, think or don't think, has an everlasting effect on eternity. Karmically, we genuinely reap in the future what we sow in the present, but in a singular, world soul version, not individually. What we do can and does affect us karmically in this life.

It should be comforting to you that, indeed, we are all part of the God organism and we therefore have a responsibility to the whole; each of us making minute by minute contributions to that energy field. It might also be disconcerting to know the negative impact others make on our universe. Surely, we are insulated from their acts by distance and time; but let there be no mistake, the energy created by actions ultimately affects the entire Universe/ God organism.

Now the question which must be burning brightly in your mind is what exactly is this energy? We know that an energy exists. Some call it the life force; some call it bioenergy; Reich called it Orgone energy. I believe that we could refer to it as God Energy or Universal Life Force Energy. I believe that that which we call "Soul" is made up of this energy, somehow captured on a cellular/nucleic/ biochemical/atomic level. One thing is for certain, most men have not been able to clearly define it in terms of its properties. Mankind in general has not been able to harness or utilize it in defined ways. We have not been able to produce it from other sources of energy or matter. It has been left to the clergy or the spiritualists to define it in terms of belief as opposed to scientific clarity.

There are some things we can say about it. It appears to be part and parcel of all organic matter. When living organisms cease to function, it appears to leave. There is a prevailing belief that it has memory, which I agree with but in a different paradigm as we will see. There seems to be an endless supply as new organisms are created and recreated from base inorganic material. In its kinetic form, when ultimately captured nucleically, it converts from kinetic energy to bioenergy, setting the organism into motion (the two definitions of life being motility and reproductivity). Living organisms recognize the departure of this energy from a loved one or mate and feel the void that's left. Some would argue that this is strictly an emotional reaction, but then what is an emotion but expressed or unexpressed energy? Beyond this, we know very little about it and appear to have no control over it.

It is this very lack of control from which man has created superstition, beliefs, and religion and appointed others to define the unknown and to reconnect us with the mystical energy of the universe. It is the devastation it wreaks when we sense its loss or disconnect and the unwillingness to accept our own roles and evolvement in the natural progress of that energy that causes us to worship icons and idols, planets and other phenomena as simple explanations. I want to make it clear that I am not against these institutions as they provide true comfort and a real buffer between the mystical and reality. I also am in no way tearing down those icons because, as we will discuss in the chapter on the God Men, there may indeed be some truth in the stories, myths, and legends of history.

I do take exception to these institutions creating negative energies that result in damage and injury to the bioenergetic source, the Anima Mendi or world soul that we are all a part of, and using these icons and legends for political or economic power and gain. They begin to outlive their usefulness for maintaining our Universe and the God Force when we are manipulated by our fears and beliefs and stampeded into destruction and pain. We therefore must accept some individual responsibility for the actions of the whole and not capitulate to the manipulation of our fears and lost connection.

"When man disassociates from this energy in the name of 'survival' that we become so vulnerable." We spend a large portion of our adult lives trying to find it again. In search of that mystical connection, we look in churches and synagogues, seek wise teachers, messiahs and gurus, make pilgrimages to far off lands, to visits to the oceans or forests, spend hours in meditations, engage in fasting, etc. What must be clearly understood is that there is no right or wrong way to Nirvana, to enlightenment, or salvation. There is no one single belief or philosophy, set of dogma, or rituals that has the patent. We must accept that each of our own methods to reconnect to the bioenergetic source, the Anima Mendi, the God Force, is just as good, just as important, just as effective as any other. It is not the path which one takes, but the destination that is paramount. We must reconnect and stay connected as much as possible, for it is in that connection, that we ultimately experience inner peace and a return to the Garden.

Barry Wachs

Rational Universalism, The Second Directive

It is my belief that we exist to evolve, to contribute to the collective God Force, to continue an ever grander spiral towards improving the quality of the Life Force/bio energetic pool to which we belong.

Chapter IV

The Justification of Existence

All organisms in the Universe evolve to their highest potential and use.

So, if all this holds true, how were we created? How can we answer this nagging question of what exactly is existence as we know it? Was there an Adam and Eve? A Garden of Eden?

I make no attempt here to dispel anybody's beliefs, as yours are just as valid as mine. However, you must agree that it all was a result of evolution, not instant creation, beyond the initial motion that propagated the Life Force. Scientists are holding onto the Big Bang theory and evolution based on what they perceive as scientific proof, while the many religious fundamentalists hold tightly onto their beliefs, based on intuition, anecdotal evidence, perhaps ancient memory, a reliance on ancient scripture, folklore, myth and superstition.

Let us reflect on my previous model for a moment. If we are all part of the God organism, the God Energy, let us make a simple assumption. Whatever that energy was, is and will be, existed before the Earth did, and will continue on whether the Earth exists in its present form or not. This energy was part of the Earth's formation, fashioned not necessarily by what we perceive or what has been commonly believed biblically, as two hands, but rather by the hands of universal creation.

Let us take another small leap and say that the conditions at the time of Earth's creation were perfect for the creation of microscopic organisms, which could trap the God Energy and convert protein into tiny building blocks we now call DNA and RNA. Whether it was a result of atmospheric pressures, temperatures, elements, or the sheer force of the creation of the planet; these minute organisms were born from the God Energy. Was it ordained, ordered, or planned? I am willing to accept the fundamental belief that perhaps there is order to the Universe, as it appears to be orderly everywhere from the atomic level to the largest galaxy. If there is an order to it all, then the God Force/Life Energy was at work here, and all living matter now became a reflection of and connected to the energy.

The law of motion is relevant here, which states that matter put into motion, stays in motion until it meets a force of equal or greater value. The creation of life was put into motion, and since the God Energy/Life Force Energy/ Universal Energy likes order, the organisms (as in organized life forms) began to evolve into their highest forms. This, I believe, is an essential truism of the God Force as well as Darwinism. All organisms in the Universe evolve to their highest potential and use, based on need and environment. If this holds true, and I believe that both faith and science agree on this principle, then we are on a continuum towards our highest potential to serve the Whole, which we call the God Force/Universal Energy/Life Force Energy, etc.

Perhaps in our ancient history, there was a mated pair, a man and woman, who lived in a land of innocence, of simplicity, who represented a major evolvement. (What scientists might call a series of mutations, I refer to as spiritual and physical evolvements.) Even if science is correct and they evolved from primordial ooze, and even if an earlier evolvement was more primitive then this mated pair(s), it makes no difference, as it was the prime directive of the Universe, of the God Force, the Universal will. We as mere mortal men recorded it and created folklore to explain it. That certainly gives us hope and faith that we are still physically and spiritually evolving; perhaps towards a new age of understanding and acceptance of our existence.

The story of Adam and Eve, as an allegorical representation, sits on the edge of creation. We recognize men's and women's biological directive for selective breeding; always searching for the best possible mate that meets our physical, mental, and spiritual criteria on an energetic level. It is my belief that we exist to evolve, to contribute to the collective God Force, to continue an ever grander spiral towards improving the quality of the Life Force/ bioenergetic pool to which we belong. Ultimately, when we pass on, our energy once again becomes one with the God Force. We will discuss this contribution in a later chapter. Even with the concept of evolution, there was no error made. It was, and is, all part of the order of the God Force/Universal Force/ Life Force for order and motion as opposed to chaos. Species have come and gone in an ever evolving existence.

In embryology, which is the study of the development of the embryo in the uterus or womb, there is a basic law: the ontogeny tends to recapitulate phylogeny. Simply put, as the embryo develops in the womb, it goes through a series of changes which mimic most of the evolutionary changes of the organism. In humans, we begin as one-celled organisms, go through a fish stage, a reptilian stage, etc., before we begin to take on the characteristics of modern man.

I believe that when we are born, our perception is that we are in the Garden of Innocence. We are taken care of, connected to the Universe energetically; and it is only after we have to assert ourselves to survive, do we begin to lose that innocence and connection. We then spend the rest of our lives trying to find it again. Some of us find it in church or synagogue, some in nature, some in romance and love. We spurn judgment by mortals and flee to find the warmth and love of a higher power, the mystical father I spoke of in my introduction. The humor of it all is that we are already part of that higher power and have chosen not to see, feel, sense or accept our own eternity. We can be thankful that the Universe/God Force has recognized this and, throughout history, has sent us <u>mortal</u> men and women with the ability to remind us, to teach us, to refocus us. We will call these mortals, the men and women of God, or God men. A discussion of their presence and mission will be looked at and appreciated separately.

Rational Universalism, The Second Directive

Upon death of our organism, our life force energy spreads throughout the Universe with all the memories, wisdom, knowledge and experience we have gathered and are there for all time and for all mankind to use and communicate with.

Chapter V

The Leap

All energy has commonality, in life and death.

We have come a long way down the path of evolution, be it by design or by random accident. It is not important to win the debate as to which is right, as we must learn now to live in the present. What is our responsibility as humans in the here and now? Do we continue to debate these issues and, if we disagree, kill, hurt, reject, and shun each other over it? In this chapter, we will take the real leap of faith that takes us to a new paradigm. We will begin to see that what we call Life Force Energy/God/Spirit/Soul is indeed energy, one which MUST follow the laws of energy through the Universe.

All energies, which we have previously identified, have common properties as well as specific characteristics that define them. Electrical energy, atomic energy, geophysical energy, etc., can be defined by their performances, temperatures, abilities to flow, etc.; but I want to focus on one common characteristic of all energy. When energy is released from its conductor or encapsulation, changes form, speeds up or slows down, it spreads simultaneously and multi-directionally.

An example might be a bathtub filled with water into which, by accident, an electrical appliance falls, and the water becomes totally electrified simultaneously and multi-directionally. All energy acts in this fashion, weather and other conditions aside. Whether from a mushroom-shaped cloud, a geyser, or a volcano, the energy spreads simultaneously and multi-directionally when released. Each has its own set of defining characteristics to be sure, but the simultaneous release in all directions is a common property.

What if we were to take that plugged-in electrical appliance and tossed it into the ocean? Yes, the electrical energy would spread from the source in every direction. It might end up blowing a fuse but, initially, it would act as it should, spreading in every direction simultaneously. How far away from the source would you feel its presence? Would it not still be there, despite distance and time?

So why is it that we humans can't conceive or understand that when we die and our Life Force Energy leaves its encapsulation that we call the brain or heart, it simply follows the laws of energy. It does not float out of the body forever formatted in some bubble or imaginary, undefined soul to be reinstalled at some future time. It does not cue up in some simplistic geographic spot in the sky to be evaluated, revamped and then sent back or doomed to an eternity of damnation. Our energy simply leaves our body (remember, energy can be a wave or a particle, and that matter cannot be created nor destroyed) and spreads simultaneously and multi-directionally throughout our known universe. Though more concentrated in the beginning, as time and distance sets in, it becomes part and parcel of a much larger pool of Life Force Energy that surrounds us; a force that we can call, if you choose to, the God Force or Life Force Energy. I suspect there are some gravitational forces at work which keeps it closer to our known earth, but this is speculation.

I am not alone in my quest. Professor Oliver Reiser of the University of Pittsburg theorized a "psi bank" which he claimed is a magnetic memory around the earth that is influencing biological evolution. It is a depository for thoughts and is held in place by electromagnetic bands around the earth. He gave it the name "Psychosphere". Dr. Telhard De Chardin, as early as 1922, recognized the "noosphere" which he felt emerges through and is constituted by the interaction of the human mind. He stated that as mankind organizes itself in complex social networks, the higher the "noosphere" will grow in awareness, growing in integration and unification. As abstract as this may sound, Princeton has been providing an ongoing study since 1998, called the Princeton Global Consciousness Project to study these and similar concepts.

Now here is another leap that I am willing to take, and it's a big one; in fact, it is the essence and nucleus of this book. That soul energy, that Life Force made up of all the memories, wisdom, knowledge, and experiences, positive and negative, good and bad, early and late, that were encapsulated within our organism and expressed as internal memory, has external memory. This is not that big a stretch from the concept of a soul with memory, floating to some unknown destination that has dominated traditional religious dogma. However, there is a difference.

This is so huge you may need to give it some thought. If my theory is correct, then all the collective memories, wisdom, knowledge, and experiences by all who ever lived in this universe surround us every moment in our lives. This opposes the concept that the soul ascends to a higher place for future storage or evaluation as a single, defined unit. Good, bad and indifferent, it is all there, the good and the evil, the Yin and Yang. This is not the Akashic records as reflected in New Age philosophy, but rather the sum total of all living memory which has existed since time began. The implications of this truth are astounding and should bring real questions to bear.

The first question that theologians might ask is, can it create and perform miracles? I believe this Universal Energy to be inert; it cannot produce, create, destroy, move, perform, in and by itself. It is there only for us to sense, read, channel, and communicate with energetically. It cannot move or create mountains, part the Red Sea, heal or do anything of and by itself. Those who communicate with it, which can be any and all of us to a greater or lesser extent, can receive advice, insight, wisdom, and knowledge from it. It is us mortals who take action, guided by the

Universal truths, wisdom and knowledge of the Life Force that has gone before us, and that manifest and create the illusion, perhaps even a delusion, of a miracle. This does not discount the miracle, just remanifests the source and the means by which it becomes a reality.

We all have the ability to sense, feel, and communicate with this Universal Life Force Energy. All living things have contributed to it. It must eventually become clear to you that all of our departed exist within this energy continuum. If that is, in fact, correct, and my theory holds true, then yes, we may be able to communicate with them on an energetic level through meditation, prayer, or nonverbal communication. They can only answer back energetically. It is your sensitivity to their energy that will allow this to take place. From a strictly anecdotal source, there may indeed be an ancestral predisposition.

What about ghosts and spirits? The human mind is an amazing tool; it can manifest and create in our conscious and unconscious mind what it needs to in order to process information. I believe that spirits, etc., are creations of our energetic minds which we develop in order to process information, communicate with the Life Force, and even create delusional sightings to provide a logical explanation for the messages, etc. A haunting is one's own method of acknowledging the energetic sensitivity to a specific soul which has been dispersed into the Life Force Energy around us. I am not discounting genetics, as it seems anecdotally to hold true that when we are related to a departed or our ancestors, our level of sensitivity to their energy appears to rise. This is only speculation but may have energetic truth.

In the next chapter, we are going to talk about the "gifts" that abound via the Life Force. We are going to explore the possibilities and how the Life Force works with genetics to create them. Within that discussion, we will examine the "Men of God" and what they were/are about.

Barry Wachs

The gift is given to every new life at conception and is part and parcel of the Universal Life force Energy that contains all the memories, wisdom, knowledge, and experiences of all who have lived before. It is beyond the genetics of the parent and has its own effect.

Chapter VI

The Gift

At conception of the fetus, a bionic joining together of the parental genetics are accompanied by a random bioenergetic fusion from the Life Force/God Force, and is the Universal gift to the child, which brings life, talents and nongenetically related behavior into it.

This "gift" is very random and can be good, bad or indifferent. It provides an explanation as to why children are born with many different talents and abilities. Talents like art, math, music, good behavior and negative behavior. When there is no genetic evidence that a given talent exists within the gene pool of the parents, I suspect it is a gift from the Universal Life Force Energy which has provided it. This is the other way that that Universal Life Force Energy, the total of all of history's knowledge, wisdom, experience, and behavior can affect us in contemporary terms.

We can enter a lengthy discussion of Nurture vs. Nature, and I as a psychologist would be the last to discount the effect of "nurture" as a way of explaining behavior. I believe that talent and behavior can, and frequently does, come from this third source; you may chose to call it part of nature, but it appears to be random and inconsistent with nature. I have given it a third identification as being gifted by the Universe.

I have never met a single person who couldn't tell you stories about two children from the same family, even twins, with the same nature and nurture background, who are so completely opposite. Perhaps psychologists can launch themselves into a long pseudo-scientific justification for these phenomena, but I feel strongly that the "gift" has much more to do with it. Remember that the bioenergy of the Universe, based on my theory, has memory, so when it enters into the bioenergetic bond at conception, it brings with it that memory, no matter how small the atomic particle. One can easily extrapolate the long-term and larger picture here. Outside of genetics, an unpredictable behavior or talent can and does appear.

From this recognition, I want to begin the discussion of the "Men of God": Abraham, Isaac, Jacob, Joseph, Moses, Buddha, Jesus, Mohammed, etc. I focus on the Men of God, but we could certainly include Joan of Arc, Sister Teresa, and perhaps many other highly evolved persons, both men and woman as well. Were they messianic? Perhaps in their way! But one thing is for sure, they were all teachers. I am of the belief that they too were born with a gift: the ability to tune into, hear, understand, interpret and teach the wisdom, knowledge and experience of the Universe from an energetic level that most men and women cannot begin to understand. Imagine a thousand voices, a million voices, speaking all at once; they were able to filter out the messages of tens of thousands of years and to make sense of it. They were able to blend all of it into a similar message was delivered to all mankind at different times in different ways. We have built icons to represent them, cathedrals to worship them, laws and rules to follow them. All they wanted was for us to hear the messages and wisdom they offered us from the Universe. Their messages of love, hope, kindness, living ethically, raising families, being the best that you can be, etc., were never meant as a reason to deify them or worship them blindly.

It was to honor the Universal Life Force Energy that contains all the memories, wisdom, knowledge, and experience of all who have gone before. They wanted us to understand that we are part and parcel of that energy, that when you leave your present form on Earth, your energy will join with all that has preceded you, and that your memories, wisdom, knowledge, and experiences will become a part of the story and history of the Universe forever. It was never to create complicated and twisted histories of their coming and going, nor to use their presence as a means to add to the manipulation and control via a theocracy. They would be appalled by it. It's counterintuitive. I am saying it would be beneficial to return to the simplicity of their teachings, nothing more, nothing less. Connect to the Universe in whatever way works best for you, be it in a church or by the sea. You don't have to build golden edifices in their honor; just following their teachings is enough.

Rational Universalism, The Second Directive

The Second Directive is the responsibility to evolve the eternal memories, wisdom, knowledge and experiences that we create in this lifetime, so that when we pass on, our legacy to the Universe is a positive, more evolved spirit/ soul/Life Force Energy.

Chapter VII

The Second Directive Revealed

We have a choice to make between evolvement of the Life Force Energy or the status quo, to live only by the prime directive or accept the challenge of changing the course and quality of the Universal Life Force Energy/God Energy.

So here we are, in the middle of this Universal energetic force, made up of all the memories, wisdom, knowledge, and experiences of all who have gone before us. I talked previously about the ability to communicate with that energy and the ability of the energy to communicate back. However, that energy cannot create in and of itself, or manifest action in our world directly. It can affect us by guidance and advice. It can affect us as we form new life in combination with the genetics of the parents and thus have a major effect on future actions and generations.

I have talked about the importance of enlightened theocracy to provide counsel and guidance, a social network, laws and rules for a civilization to live with one another. I talked about the initial reasons for faith and science as a means by which the common man can make sense out of the chaos of the unknown and unanswered.

This allows us to return to the innocent state of connection to the Universal Life Force/God Force with which we are originally born and then lose as we struggle to survive in a harsh world. We have assigned shamans/ministers/religious leaders to assist us periodically as we need to connect. Many of these leaders have heretofore frequently used the fear of the unknown to manipulate and control us in conjunction with the political leaders with which they have formed theocracies. We are left with an interesting irony. We have choices to make as to how we relate to the Universe and to the God/Life Force.

For thousands of years we have carried out the Prime Directive. It is the same for all species on earth: survive and procreate. We all must continue the species at whatever the cost. This includes the cost of destroying other species to extinction in the name of survival. Only man has developed the ability to reason and to make conscious decisions about his actions; all other species act primarily on instinct and reflex. (We don't know about the dolphins and whales.) We are the only species that can put instinct aside and analyze it. We are the only species that works consciously on a spiritual level with our own "soul or spirit," and creates deities to worship with hopes that they can affect or change the real world.

We can analyze our experiences in a spiritual world as opposed to just reacting to them reflexively. (Some of the other primates can analyze and make decisions, but not on a spiritual plane.) Along with this ability to reason, to analyze, and to recognize the need to make a spiritual connection, comes the ability to make conscious decisions about what we choose to learn, retain and put into our memory banks. We are capable of controlling our experiences to a great extent, as in what wisdom or path we choose to follow and, thus, absorb into our being. This is the concept of The Second Directive.

What will be our ultimate legacy to the world? What will we leave behind and contribute to the Universal Life Force/God Force? We can make conscious decisions to leave a more highly evolved energy for all time, or not. We can live each day, making major decisions based on the concept of evolution of the spirit, or we can just live our lives in an ethical and honorable way, by loving, caring, raising our families, doing the least harm to others, accepting people and situations, reducing our judgment of others, which would automatically evolve the energy. We can choose to remain in survival mode and be defensive, reactive, greed filled, intimidating, manipulative, power hungry, dismissive, controlling, and ultimately Ego driven.

I would like to end the discussion of the Second Directive by addressing the concept of absolution. Absolution is an act of forgiveness which is given by a priest at confession, by a Rabbi at Yom Kippur, by a minister from his pulpit, etc. It is only through absolution that one religion can justify killing a member of another, because they have been told they will be forgiven or even rewarded. The act of Absolution has caused some Christians to kill Jews, some

Rational Universalism, The Second Directive

Jews to kill Moslems, some Moslems to kill Infidels, etc. Because we foster the belief that we can be forgiven by our clergy or deity in the name of our religion, that we can act in violence without carrying the guilt we deserve. Whenever a violent act is perpetrated upon another living thing, be it mayhem, violence or murder, the negative energy that occurs around the incident cannot be pulled back, erased or eradicated from history or from one's own energetic memory banks. We ultimately must be responsible for what we do to others. You may be given forgiveness and absolution in this life, but you will always carry that act for all eternity within your atomic, energetic memory and will be part of your eternal legacy.

What does an evolved energy look like? What does it act like? How can we describe it? This is not an easy question because many philosophies, existing beliefs and faiths, feel they have a corner on the definition, "Their way or no way." You must follow their rules and paths to enlightenment or acceptance or salvation. If you really take a good look at most faiths and beliefs in the world, there are some common qualities that can define "decent living." Those qualities include love, kindness, caring, living in the present; raising a family with love, without paranoia, suspicion and distrust; being conscious of the earth and its fragility; not committing murder, mayhem, theft, or destruction of other's property; having consideration for your fellow man; not judging others for their behavior, appearance or beliefs; and lastly, not judging yourself or others too harshly for not always doing the right thing. We are imperfect; and as such, we will input data into our memory banks that is not always good and great and wonderful. We will err, hurt and damage someone or something. Learning to forgive yourself and others, in and of itself, is part of the evolution of your spirit.

We and the Universe are works in progress. Live with that sense of eternal evolution of the Life Force, the God Force, what our legacy to it will be, and it all begins makes sense.

Rational Universalism, The Second Directive

Within the scope of this text, a new paradigm, a new vision of the God Spirit/Universal Life Force Energy emerges. A vision of a God Force, not aimed at providing guilt or fear of reprisal or punishment from the God Force/Life Force itself, but only from the knowledge that the legacy you provide to the God Force/Life Force upon death, is there for all eternity. This will be your undeniable contribution to the Eternal memories, wisdom, knowledge, experiences that you have created. Only you have the ability to determine the quality and nature of that legacy; use it wisely. This is the application of Rational Universalism; this is the Second Directive.

Chapter VIII

The Do's and Doesn'ts

In the larger scheme of things, the concept of Rational Universalism and The Second Directive shifts the source of many beliefs, but is not intended to destroy or eliminate them.

As we analyze this new theory of the Universal Life Force Energy/God Energy, it does several things to existing beliefs and also does not do many things to existing systems. In the larger scheme of things, the concept of Rational Universalism and The Second Directive shifts the source of many beliefs, but is not intended to destroy or eliminate them in any way.

Let me begin with what Rational Universalism does not do. By that I mean, what it does not do to existing faiths and beliefs. It does not ask any faith to change the way it makes the ultimate connection to the God Force/Universal Life Force Energy. It does not ask anyone to put aside rituals and rites, the means by which, perhaps for thousands of years, faiths have acknowledged the existence of the God Force. It does not ask that they cease to pray to it, turn to it for guidance and advice, ask it for action in their lives (even in the face of an inert Energy Force that can only guide and advise). It does not ask anyone to put aside whatever icons and structures have been created to represent and house their beliefs and faiths. It does not ask that theocracies self destruct or cease to exist, but only become enlightened. By enlightened, I mean they are not critical to other beliefs for taking a different path, accept evolution as a proven scientific fact within the definition of doing the work of the God Force, and accept a nonevangelical method of expanding their followers. They understand that all faiths lead to the same mountain top. It does not ask that faiths and belief systems quit taking responsibility for teaching ethics, culture, and lifestyles (as long as it does no harm to others). It does not ask that the essential social interaction of people with like minds be dissolved, including charity, support, counseling and the pure sense of community. It does not ask that faiths put aside their myths, folklore, oral histories, historical enhancements and exaggerations in oral or written form, as long as they do no harm to others in the name of those myths, etc. by manipulation or misinterpretation. It does not ask that you abandon the concept that all life was started by a higher power; that is a matter of pure faith, but that once life began, in whatever form it may have taken and by whatever force, it began the evolutionary process.

What it does do is redefine the form of the God Spirit from an entity with human-like emotions such as happiness, sadness, anger, frustration, jealousy, humor (which only meets our collective human ego enhancement) into a collective energy, the Life Force Energy/God Energy, which surrounds us for all eternity. This concept asks that you acknowledge the obvious evolution of the species on a physical and intellectual level based on Darwinian Evolution, and put aside the artificial antagonist and conflict created by those in power to manipulate and control. It acknowledges that we are not only evolving as a physical species, but spiritually as well. It asks that you put aside traditional views of reincarnation, Heaven and Hell, etc., and replace it with an understanding that our soul/spirit energies pass into the vast Universal Energy Force with its memories, wisdom, knowledge, and experiences to be shared by all throughout eternity. It asks that you put aside fear of punishment by the God Force and understand it is your own guilt and sense of the legacy you give to the Life Force/God Force that determines your behavior and how you will be judged by those left behind. The God Force/Universal Life Force does not have the power or the ability to directly create or make things happen. It can only advise and guide the living, who in turn can create and manifest concepts, ideas and actions. The God Force/Universal Life Force will always be there for our use, advice, guidance, knowledge, including relatives, family, ancestors, etc. who have passed.

Lastly, it asks that you consider the possibility that you may take conscientious actions to evolve the Life Force. You can choose to take actions beyond simply living that evolve the Life Force/God Force Energy to even greater heights. This action includes any and all positive actions from charity to giving love, caring, understanding, volunteering, etc. This is the Second Directive: to take individual responsibility for the positive evolution of the God Force/Universal Life Force in whatever way works in your life and to embrace the concept of living gracefully and lovingly to your best extent. Nothing more, nothing less.

Barry Wachs

The Beginning, not the end.

Chapter IX

Synthesis

We can now take responsibility for ourselves and our own actions

So far, I have deconstructed traditional religious models and, at the same time, have acknowledged that we all have the right and indeed the need to connect on some level with the Life Force/God Force in some way. I have encouraged you to continue with your sacredness in whatever way you chose to worship, with the understanding that you do no harm to others, or use your faith to manipulate and control as a power over others.

I have clearly stated that guilt need not come from fear of punishment or reward from an unknown entity, as that is nothing more than a transfer of past (usually patriarchal) parental control over our infantile belief that we need an entity in our lives that is omnipotent and present in order to prevent us from doing the wrong things and to reward us for doing the right and righteous. The truth is that a healthy, integrated mind can create healthy controls over its own behavior based on the laws and ethics of the society in which it lives.

Rational Universalism, The Second Directive

Here is where I integrate the two concepts. If you accept my theory that, when we pass from our human form, our personal energies (made up of our memories, wisdom, knowledge, and experiences) leave our bodies and are dispersed slowly throughout the Universe and are retained within the Earth's gravitational field; this becomes the ground upon which we can now base our conscious choices of behavior. This energy can be, and is constantly, updated and evolves while we live. What passes into the Universal pool made up of millions of dispersed souls (energy) that have passed before us, can and does contribute to the evolution of the Life Force/God Force. It is this understanding that allows us to consider our actions while we live in this physical form. I pose this question to you: What do you want your legacy to the God Force to be? What are you willing to do, feel, experience, learn, or behave, that will make up your legacy? We each become our own judge and jury. In this model, our own guilt, pride or joy about how we have lived our lives is sufficient. We don't need a patriarchal or parental super-spiritual entity to fear or to please. We can now take responsibility for ourselves and our own actions.

So now we acknowledge the presence of the Life Force/God Force around us. It is this force we sense in nature, during prayer, meditation or in periods of awareness and enlightenment. It is the presence of this force that provides guidance and advice to us, perhaps more so from family and ancestors that have passed as a result of a bioenergetic bond which may exist. It is important to note that this energy is inert; it cannot perform, create, take physical action, perform miracles, but can merely guide and advise us to take action, etc.

With the concepts of the Second Directive, which states that we have the choice to evolve the Universal Life Force/God Force Energy by our individual actions, memories, wisdom, knowledge and experiences which we collect within our own energy during life, can we begin to build a better Universe, a loving world, a healthy Universal consciousness. It is our own individual evolution, growth, awareness, etc. that expands the evolution of the Life Force/God Force. You can choose to make a difference, remain neutral or even add negatively to it. Let there be no doubt that whatever you choose, you will own for eternity. There will be no second chances, returns to earth to redo your choices, or ways of making amends. What you collect within your energy will be your legacy. You will possess it as part of your contribution to the Life Force/ God Force forever. Choose wisely.

Lastly, the pool of Life Force/God Force energy exists all around us with memory. We can connect to it through prayer, meditation, etc.; and at the moment of conception of the new fetus, an atomic/molecular bond takes place with the fetus and a particle of universal memory which creates behavior, life, and talents. It is what theologians might call the spark of life or of God. This atomic bond is random, bioenergetic and irreversible. If this is true, then again, the quality of the energy pool is important in the evolution of the species.

I am hopeful that the theory I have posed in this book is not the end, but rather the beginning of a new paradigm in the concepts of the Life Force/God Force. I am hopeful that others might find truths and inspiration which thrust them into further exploration. I have purposely avoided discussions on how to worship or honor the Directive, as I did not want to create another basis for iconoclastic worship, but rather a framework upon which you can continue your present worship and sacred acknowledgement of the Life Force/God Force through a different lens, perhaps with a renewed zest for what you already know, along with a new tool and reason to bolster your dedication. I encourage you to honor your previous teachings and rituals and add to them the concepts of the Second Directive, with humility and love.

Barry Wachs, a flawed and evolving energy.

Barry Wachs

About the Author

Born in 1944 in the Bronx, New York, like so many East Coast Jews, Barry Wachs, PhD, had a mother who was off the boat from Hungary, and a father who was first generation Russian, rousted from their quaint lives in small Eastern European Villages by the forces of anti-Semitic sentiment that prevailed all over Europe at the time. His mother worked in a sweat shop sewing clothes for pennies and his father worked with his own father buying and selling potato sacks from a horse drawn carriage in Connecticut. Ultimately his parents married and had 3 children. Barry was the youngest, and at age two, his family was drawn to the Golden land of California where his father was assisted into business by a relative which lasted 23 years.

Barry attended school in an ethnically mixed community of Southwest Los Angeles, and after graduating from high school, attended University of Southern California (USC), majoring in Premed. He ended up going to The Los Angeles College of Chiropractic in Glendale, Ca. Upon graduation in 1967, he then proceeded to practice Chiropractic for 24 yours. During that time, Barry was attracted to a special off campus program at the University of California at L.A. which was an experimental campus. One of the programs offered was a Doctorate program in Reichian psychology, which he attended for 3 years, wrote a doctoral thesis and was awarded a PhD in psychology with an emphasis on the works of Wilhelm Reich.

Over the years, like any good psychologist, Barry has explored many theories and approaches to the behaviors of man, including the work of Jung, Pearls, Parkinson, and Neurolinguistic programming. He is a certified Clinical hypnotherapist, and attributes much of his insight to the work of David Quiggly. He was licensed in Arizona for over 20 years as a naturopathic physician. His curiosity has taken him far beyond Judaism, and has studied numerous religions and beliefs, and has delved into behavior of hundreds of patients over the years.

Barry's other work includes 14 years as a Vocational Rehabilitation Counselor and a therapist in a major acute mental/psychiatric hospital. He presently practices as a holistic, alternative health practitioner in Citrus Heights, California and is listed in *Who's Who in California*.

www.ingramcontent.com/pod-product-compliance
Lightning Source LLC
LaVergne TN
LVHW011430080426
835512LV00005B/359